BOUNCING BACK FROM EXTINCTION

THE RETURN OF THE MOUNTAIN GORILLA

SARAH MACHAJEWSKI

PowerKiDS press™

New York

Published in 2018 by The Rosen Publishing Group, Inc.
29 East 21st Street, New York, NY 10010

First Edition

Editor: Theresa Morlock
Book Design: Reann Nye

Photo Credits: Cover Thomas Marent/Visuals Unlimted, Inc./Getty Images; p. 4 Smileus/Shutterstock.com; p. 5 (Pyrenean ibex) dragoms/Moment Open/Getty Images; pp. 5 (jaguar), 17 Travel Stock/Shutterstock.com; p. 5 (Arctic fox, hippopotamus) bikeriderlondon/Shutterstock.com; p. 5 (orangutan) Sergey Uryadnikov/Shutterstock.com; p. 5 (Wyoming toad) https://commons.wikimedia.org/wiki/File:Bufo_baxteri-3.jpg; p. 7 Eric Gevaert/Shutterstock.com; p. 8 Suha Derbent/Shutterstock.com; p. 9 David Pluth/National Geographic/Getty Images; p. 10 Eric Kruszewski/National Geographic Magazines/Getty Images; p. 11 Mary Ann McDonald/Shutterstock.com; p. 12 Simon Eeman/Shutterstock.com; pp. 13, 27 GUDKOV ANDREY/Shutterstock.com; p. 15 David Cayless/Photolibrary/Getty Images; p. 16 pingebat/Shutterstock.com; p. 18 Liba Taylor/Corbis Documentary/Getty Images; p. 19 FCG/Shutterstock.com; pp. 20, 21 Brent Stirton/Getty Images News/Getty Images; p. 22 Anup Shah/Corbis Documentary/Getty Images; p. 23 United News/Popperfoto/Getty Images; pp. 24, 29 LMspencer/Shutterstock.com; p. 25 Thierry Falise/LightRocket/Getty Images; p. 28 zampe238/Shutterstock.com; p. 30 ForeverLee/Shutterstock.com.

Cataloging-in-Publication Data

Names: Machajewski, Sarah.
Title: The return of the mountain gorilla / Sarah Machajewski.
Description: New York : PowerKids Press, 2018. | Series: Bouncing back from extinction | Includes index.
Identifiers: ISBN 9781508156222 (pbk.) | ISBN 9781508156154 (library bound) | ISBN 9781508156031 (6 pack)
Subjects: LCSH: Gorilla–Juvenile literature. | Endangered species–Juvenile literature.
Classification: LCC QL737.P96 M33 2018 | DDC 599.884–dc23

Manufactured in the United States of America

CPSIA Compliance Information: Batch #BS17PK: For Further Information contact Rosen Publishing, New York, New York at 1-800-237-9932

CONTENTS

GENTLE BEASTS

High in the mountains of Africa, large beasts with long, black hair and gentle eyes quietly walk among the trees. There's no mistaking these animals and the towering presence that shows just how powerful they are: they're mountain gorillas.

Mountain gorillas are amazing creatures. They're extremely strong but generally calm. In many ways, they behave like people. They live together in groups and have a **complex** social structure in which every gorilla has a role to play. They're intelligent and can even learn sign language.

Sadly, we were once very close to a world without mountain gorillas. They have been so badly harmed by human activity that the **species** almost died out—but their story doesn't end there. Today, mountain gorilla populations are bouncing back thanks to conservation efforts.

Mountain gorillas are currently listed as a critically endangered species.

CONSERVATION STATUS CHART

EXTINCT
Having no living members.

Pyrenean ibex

EXTINCT IN THE WILD
Living members only in captivity.

Wyoming toad

CRITICALLY ENDANGERED
At highest risk of becoming extinct.

Sumatran orangutan

ENDANGERED VULNERABLE
High risk of extinction in the wild.

hippopotamus

NEAR THREATENED
Likely to become endangered soon.

jaguar

LEAST CONCERN
Lowest risk of endangerment.

Arctic fox

CLOSE RELATIVES

Mountain gorillas are mammals. They belong to a group of animals called primates. Primates have hands, handlike feet, flat nails, and eyes that face forward. Monkeys, apes, tarsiers, and lemurs are part of this group. Humans are primates, too. Gorillas share a common **ancestor** with all of these animals. If you see gorillas at the zoo, you may think they remind you of people. Now you know why!

The largest living primate is the eastern gorilla. Mountain gorillas are a subspecies of the eastern gorilla. Eastern lowland gorillas, more commonly called Grauer's gorillas, are the other subspecies. "Subspecies" means they're very closely related, but scientists put mountain gorillas into their own group

ALL ABOUT CONSERVATION

Conservation is the protection of the **environment**. It includes all aspects of the natural world, including land, water, plants, and animals. Conservation efforts help preserve the environment and its resources so we can enjoy them for years to come. Conservationists are people who work to protect the environment. But you don't have to be a professional—anyone can be a conservationist, even you!

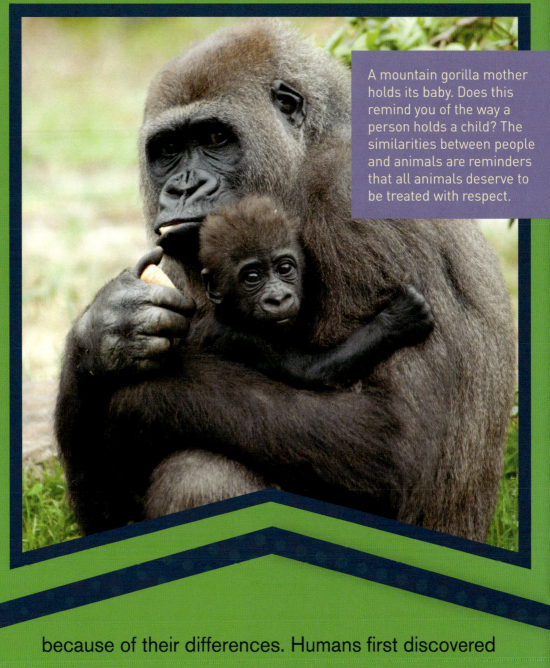

A mountain gorilla mother holds its baby. Does this remind you of the way a person holds a child? The similarities between people and animals are reminders that all animals deserve to be treated with respect.

because of their differences. Humans first discovered that the mountain gorilla was a subspecies of eastern gorillas in 1902.

THE GORILLA LIFESTYLE

The mountain gorillas' **habitat** covers a small area that belongs to three African countries: the Democratic Republic of the Congo, Rwanda, and Uganda. They live high in the mountains, between 8,000 and 13,000 feet (2,438 and 3,962 m) above sea level. The forests are very dense, or thick, in these areas. Mountain gorillas can climb trees, but they usually walk on the ground and nest in plants and leaves.

THE GORILLA DIET

The thick forests of Africa provide plenty of food for mountain gorillas. These creatures are herbivores, which means they eat plants. They eat stems of vines, shrubs, herbs, bamboo, and fruit. They also eat roots and tree bark. Mountain gorillas eat parts of up to 142 different plant species. An adult male gorilla can eat up to 40 pounds (18 kg) of plants per day!

Can you see how the silverback gorilla got its name?

Mountain gorillas have long, black fur. Adult males have a patch of silver hair on their back, which is why they're sometimes called silverbacks. Males can be up to 6 feet (1.8 m) tall and weigh up to 400 pounds (181.4 kg). Females are a bit smaller. They can grow to 5 feet (1.5 m) tall and weigh around 215 pounds (97.5 kg).

A TROOP OF GORILLAS

Mountain gorillas live in groups called troops. Troops have a complex social order. The silverback is the most **dominant** gorilla in the troop. It's often referred to as the "alpha male." Its job is to lead and protect the troop. When the alpha male feels challenged or **threatened**, it may pound its chest, roar, or throw things. The alpha

A gorilla troop is like a family. Members eat, sleep, and travel together. It's the silverback's job to protect everyone.

male dedicates his life to protecting his troop, sometimes fighting to the death to ensure their safety.

A number of females, young, and several other males round out a troop. Gorillas communicate in several different ways. They vocalize, or make different kinds of sounds with their mouth. They also touch and groom each other to communicate. Body movements and facial expressions are other ways gorillas "talk" to each other.

Female gorillas only give birth to one baby at a time. This is one of the reasons their populations are at risk. If too many gorillas die before more are born, their population decreases.

For such a large animal, mountain gorillas are born very small. Newborn gorillas only weigh about 4 pounds (1.8 kg)! After they're born, baby mountain gorillas cling to their mother's fur. When they're around four months old, baby gorillas begin to ride on their mother's back. They do this until they're two or three years old.

Mountain gorillas can live a long time. It's up to humans to be sure these gorillas get the chance to live out their lives in peace.

Young mountain gorillas always seem to be having fun. They play, climb trees, swing from branches, and chase each other. Gorillas reach adulthood when they're about 10 years old, and they live for about 40 to 50 years.

GORILLAS AT RISK

Whether people are wondering at mountain gorillas' striking similarities to humans or fearing them as dangerous enemies, these creatures have truly captured people's imaginations. Studying their gentle nature, playfulness, and awe-inspiring power has taught us a lot about the species—and ourselves. Sadly, humans have caused these creatures much suffering. Due to human actions, scientists once **predicted** that mountain gorillas would be extinct by the end of the 20th century.

However, mountain gorillas haven't gone extinct. Today, scientists think there are around 880 mountain gorillas living in the wild. There aren't any living in **captivity**. This population is higher than it once was, which is why some people say the mountain gorilla population is bouncing back. However, mountain gorillas are still critically endangered.

A NOMAD'S LIFE

Mountain gorillas are nomadic. That means that they roam around, traveling and sleeping in different places rather than staying in one spot. Mountain gorillas only travel within a range of 10 to 15 square miles (26 to 39 sq km). Every night, mountain gorillas make themselves new nests. Nests are made of branches and grass.

Mountain gorillas have been at risk since people first discovered them.

Three main factors have had a **devastating** effect on the mountain gorilla population: habitat loss, hunting, and war. Habitat loss is the loss of livable land due to changes in the environment. The land can no longer provide everything a creature needs to survive. The environment may not be a safe place to raise young. It may not have any food sources or clean water. When this happens, animals have fewer places to call home.

Democratic Republic of the Congo

Bwindi Impenetrable National Park

Uganda

Virunga mountain range

Rwanda

mountain gorilla territory

Africa

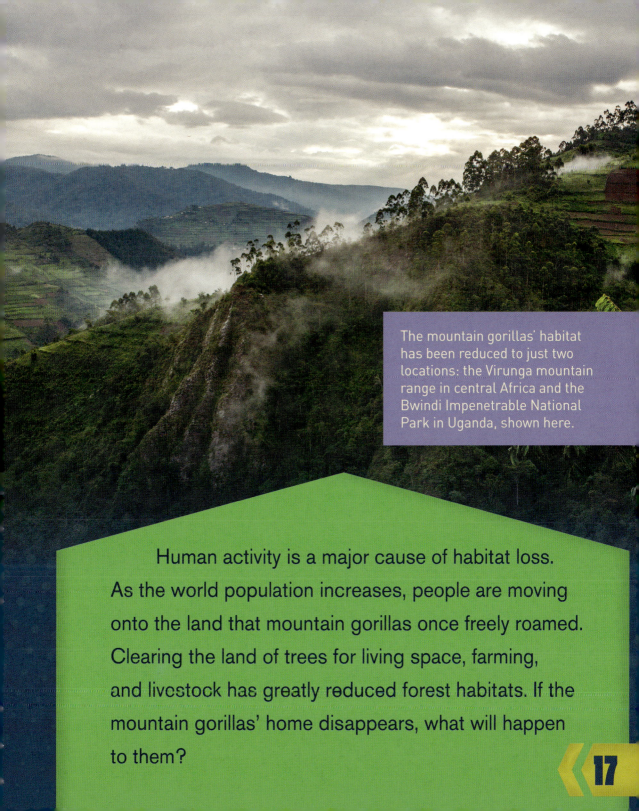

The mountain gorillas' habitat has been reduced to just two locations: the Virunga mountain range in central Africa and the Bwindi Impenetrable National Park in Uganda, shown here.

Human activity is a major cause of habitat loss. As the world population increases, people are moving onto the land that mountain gorillas once freely roamed. Clearing the land of trees for living space, farming, and livestock has greatly reduced forest habitats. If the mountain gorillas' home disappears, what will happen to them?

IN THE CROSSFIRE OF WAR

Habitat destruction can happen quickly if world events cause people to move in large numbers. War is one such event that has directly affected mountain gorillas.

In the 1990s, Rwanda experienced years of unrest and war. People were forced to leave their homes, and thousands fled to the forests of the Virunga Mountains. **Refugees** set up camps in the forests and cut down

Refugee camps like the one pictured here were set up near mountain gorillas' forest homes. This put major stress on the environment.

War doesn't just affect people. As the mountain gorillas' story shows, what we do affects the creatures that share our planet.

trees. Gorillas were exposed to human sicknesses such as measles, which can kill them. However, park rangers and conservation groups worked to help the gorillas and gave them medicine. Most importantly, they educated people. Rangers and activists taught people how important it is to protect mountain gorillas. Their efforts helped mountain gorillas survive years of war.

HUNTED

Governments make rules that say what animals people are allowed to hunt, where people can hunt, and when people can hunt. Sometimes people don't follow the rules. Poaching is the act of killing animals illegally.

Mountain gorillas have been victims of poaching. According to the World Wildlife Foundation, as many as 15 Virunga mountain gorillas may have been killed since 1990. Poachers may hunt gorillas for trophies or meat.

IN COLD BLOOD

In 2007, seven mountain gorillas were killed in Virunga National Park. News of the killings shocked and outraged people around the world. These killings may have been carried out by people who were angry that they couldn't cut down the forests where gorillas live. The killings were a political message with tragic consequences.

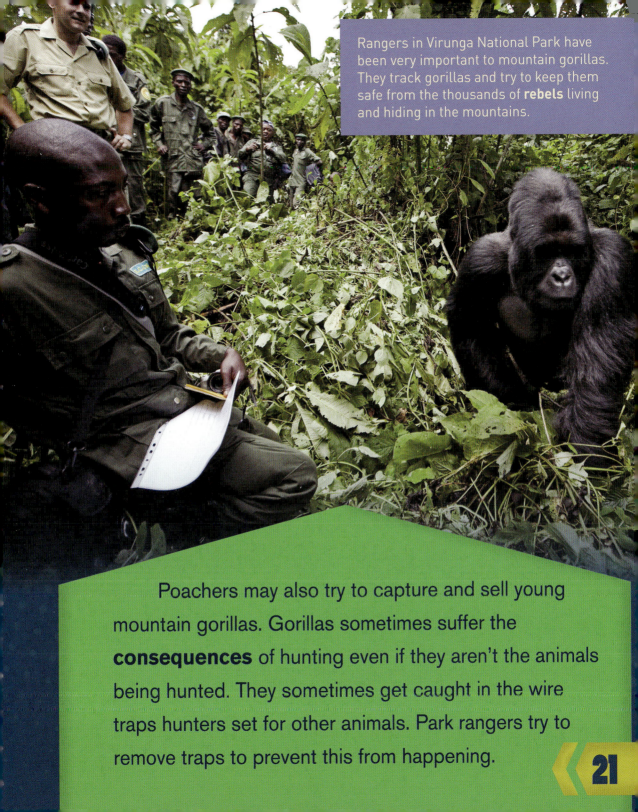

Rangers in Virunga National Park have been very important to mountain gorillas. They track gorillas and try to keep them safe from the thousands of **rebels** living and hiding in the mountains.

Poachers may also try to capture and sell young mountain gorillas. Gorillas sometimes suffer the **consequences** of hunting even if they aren't the animals being hunted. They sometimes get caught in the wire traps hunters set for other animals. Park rangers try to remove traps to prevent this from happening.

DIAN FOSSEY

Mountain gorillas would probably be extinct if not for the efforts of conservationist Dian Fossey. Fossey was an American scientist who changed the way the world thought about mountain gorillas.

With encouragement from scientist Louis Leakey, Fossey set up a research camp in the Virunga Mountains in Rwanda in 1967. At the time, people viewed mountain gorillas as **aggressive** and violent. Fossey was the

A LASTING LEGACY

Dian Fossey's work lives on decades after her death. The Dian Fossey Gorilla Fund International is a conservation group that's dedicated to helping mountain gorillas, as well as the people who live near their habitats. This group works against poachers, educates the local population, addresses health issues of gorillas and people, and more.

In 1985, Dian Fossey was found dead in her cabin in Africa. Many people think she was killed by the poachers she worked to stop. She put her own life at risk to help save mountain gorillas.

first person to get close enough to gorillas to truly understand them. She was patient and gentle and imitated their behaviors, **mimicking** their calls and movements. She gained their trust and was able to observe their lives and social order. Unfortunately she faced poachers and hunters who killed the creatures she came to love. Fossey's work drew attention to mountain gorillas, which may have saved them from extinction.

CONSERVATION EFFORTS

Starting in the late 1970s, conservationists made an effort to bring attention to mountain gorillas. They presented hard facts, such as how the Virunga mountain gorilla population fell from 275 in 1971 to 254 just 10 years later. They taught locals, including law enforcement officials, why conservation is important.

Conservationists also worked directly with gorillas. They gave them medicine and care. They worked with

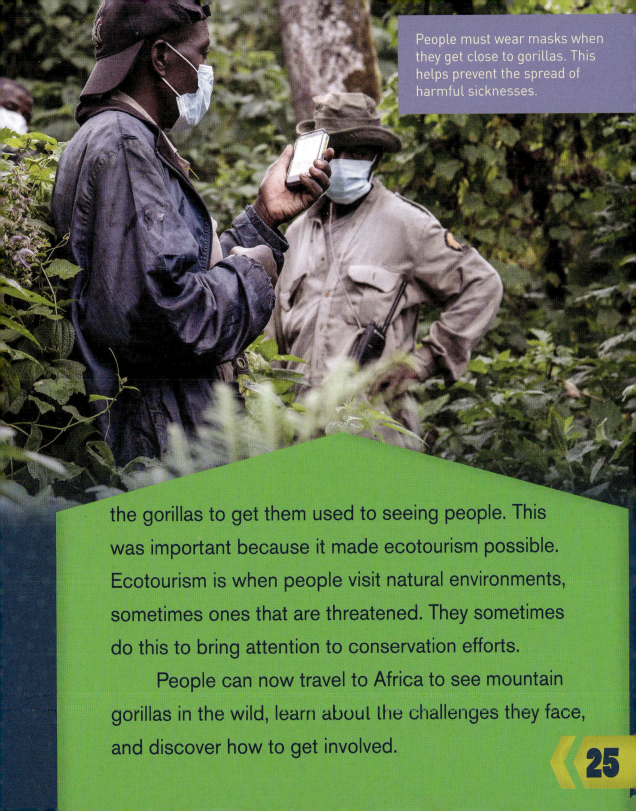

People must wear masks when they get close to gorillas. This helps prevent the spread of harmful sicknesses.

the gorillas to get them used to seeing people. This was important because it made ecotourism possible. Ecotourism is when people visit natural environments, sometimes ones that are threatened. They sometimes do this to bring attention to conservation efforts.

People can now travel to Africa to see mountain gorillas in the wild, learn about the challenges they face, and discover how to get involved.

WHAT CAN YOU DO?

You may feel like mountain gorillas are too far away to help. That's not true at all! Today, it's easier than ever for kids to get involved.

Several conservation groups work to help mountain gorillas. Some even help more than one kind of animal. You can choose to donate to these groups, which use donations to carry out their conservation efforts.

But the best way to help is to raise awareness. Ask important questions, such as: "Why is it important to protect animals of our world?" People must learn to value animals' lives. Changing someone's mindset begins with education. If you get involved now, one day we may live in a world that's safe and healthy for all creatures.

Mountain gorillas need our help!

MAKING A BRIGHTER FUTURE

As world populations continue to grow, more land is taken over, and nations remain at war, mountain gorillas still feel the consequences of our actions. However, brave people have stepped in to help mountain gorillas. Conservationists, lawmakers, and everyday people have worked hard to save these gentle giants, and their efforts have been successful.

Baby gorillas need extra protection. More gorilla babies will mean more gorillas in the future!

The mountain gorilla population dropped dangerously low in the 1980s. Today, it has grown to around 880. The biggest threats to the current population are human sicknesses, traps, and habitat loss. Conservationists are also worried that oil companies may hurt gorilla habitats. One thing is clear: mountain gorillas are still a **fragile** species. It's our job to help them—today, tomorrow, and well into the future.

GORILLAS THROUGH HISTORY

1902 People learn of the mountain gorilla subspecies.

Dian Fossey sets up a research camp in Rwanda to study mountain gorillas. **1967**

1971 The Virunga mountain gorilla population is recorded at 275.

The Virunga mountain gorilla population falls to 254. **1981**

1985 Dian Fossey is killed, possibly by poachers, at her camp in Africa.

A civil war takes place in Rwanda, compromising mountain gorillas' survival. **1990—1993**

2007 Seven mountain gorillas are killed in Virunga National Park.

The mountain gorilla population is estimated to be around 880. **2016**

GLOSSARY

aggressive: Showing a readiness to attack.

ancestor: An animal that lived before others in its family tree.

captivity: The state of being confined.

complex: Having many parts.

consequence: Something that happens as a result of a certain action or set of conditions.

devastating: Very damaging.

dominant: The most powerful or strongest.

environment: The natural surroundings for a person, plant, or animal.

fragile: Easily damaged.

habitat: The natural home for a plant or animal.

mimic: To imitate.

predict: To guess what will happen in the future based on facts or knowledge.

rebel: A person who is fighting against their government.

refugee: A person who has been forced to leave their home to escape danger.

species: A group of plants or animals that are all the same kind.

threatened: In danger.

INDEX

WEBSITES

Due to the changing nature of Internet links, PowerKids Press has developed an online list of websites related to the subject of this book. This site is updated regularly. Please use this link to access the list: www.powerkidslinks.com/bbe/gorilla